Evelyn Wood

Published by Too-Woo.com

ISBN: 978-0-9934145-2-7

EXPLORING WITH TOO WOO

The busy world of Bees

This book belongs to

....

A present from

....

DEDICATION

This book is for my friends

Margit Eichstedlund & Lis Markussen

Who have given me years of support and encouragement.

ACKNOWLEDGEMENTS

I am indebted to my wife, Aselle, who made many valuable suggestions whilst patiently proofreading and editing the various versions of this work.

I am grateful to Ellen Miller of the West Plains Beekeepers Association and Sue Mitchell of Bee-equipment Ltd for their kind generosity in answering questions that puzzled me.

I have consulted many sources, both printed and web, in writing this book. I have crosschecked information, sometimes, a dozen times. Although this small book is not meant to be scientific, I have tried to make it accurate – any errors are entirely mine. There is a list of useful books and websites on page 32.

Dictionaries used are: Oxford English, Cambridge Advanced Learners, Miriam Webster, Dictionary.com, Origins Etymological Dictionary of Modern English, The Online Etymology Dictionary and the American Heritage Dictionary.

Also by Evelyn Wood in the Exploring with Too Woo series:

The magical world of butterflies (Published 2015)

Reviews of the magical world of butterflies:

This is a great book with a fun story, fun characters and great activities and lessons! The lessons are fun for kids and give a great deal of insight into the world of butterflies. There are pages for coloring, a little quiz and a place for note taking. There are several anatomically accurate colored illustrations on every page that keep it interesting and give kids something to look at, but also help them learn by providing visual depictions of the facts presented in the story.
Tim Johnson, Author Bosley bear language books.

An entertaining and informative look at butterflies and their world. This short book provides a wealth of information in an easy to read way. A short quiz allows you to test your recently acquired knowledge and there is ample opportunity for those who like drawing and colouring in to indulge themselves. The book is filled with charming illustrations and would be an ideal introduction to the wonderful world of nature for young children.
H. T. Davies

I bought this for my 8-year-old son who thoroughly enjoyed it and found myself also learning all sorts of interesting facts. My son found the illustrations and activities engaging and we have recommended it to friends of ours who have also had fun with this informative book. A must buy for anyone with little ones that love nature and animals!
Mrs. K. Hattan

From Goodreads:

The Magical World of Butterflies really lives up to its name. It is a lovely easy reading book for school aged children as well as adults. The pictures are great and the information is really good. If the rest of the series are as good, I want them all.
If you are interested in learning more about the life of Butterflies, this is a fun way to learn.
Maddona.

Butterflies are one of my most favorite things. What an adorable book. Written for both young and old alike. I thought it was excellent. Great job!
Barbara

It is very good and educational. I thought it deserved to be in a classroom so I sent it to a friend who teaches 3rd grade. He said all the children were enjoying it too. I recommend this book highly!
Pamela

EXPLORING WITH TOO WOO

The busy world of Bees

Written and Illustrated by

Evelyn Wood

TOO WOO and the busy world of Bees

I'm Too Woo and this is the story of Bees. Without bees, we would be very hungry. This tiny insect keeps our world buzzing along.

Learn about different types of bees. How an egg hatches in its cell and grows into a bee that makes honey and helps organise life in the hive. There are some neat facts, new words and how to say them.

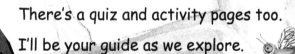

There's a quiz and activity pages too.

I'll be your guide as we explore.

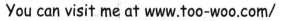

You can visit me at www.too-woo.com/

Do you know The tiny bee is one of the most important creatures on earth. Bees make honey by collecting nectar from flowers. They gather pollen too, and this fertilises the plants they visit. The plants grow fruit, vegetables, nuts or seeds. We harvest them and use the produce for food, drinks, herbs, oils and fabric.

These are just a few of the things we eat (and drink) thanks to bees and other insects.   Almonds, Brazil nuts, Cashew and Macadamia nuts. Alfalfa, Avocado, Buckwheat, Canola, Cocoa, Coffee, Cucumber, Eggplant, Pumpkin, Squash, Tomatoes and Turnips.   Apples, Blackberries, Blueberries, Cherries, Kiwifruit, Mangos, Melons, Oranges, Peaches, Passion fruit, Pears, Plums, Raspberries and Watermelon.

Scientists think that bees pollinate (fertilise) about 225,000 species of flowering plants. Without them our world would not be so colourful or smell as nice and there would be much less to eat. Without bees many people and animals would starve.

Humans have been collecting honey for thousands of years. This picture is a 10,000 year old cave painting from Spain. He must have been stung a lot stealing the honey!

Over 4,000 years ago, in Egypt, the first beekeeper discovered how to make bees live in a man-made hive. The idea spread to Greece, Rome and the rest of the world. Honey was so prized by our ancestors that the Romans even had a goddess of honey called Mellona.

Do you know that bees help make your jeans and T-shirts?

Bees play a vital role in producing food and they pollinate cotton too!

Of the 25,000 known species of bees worldwide, only 7 are Honeybees and 250 are Bumblebees. The other 24,743 are bees you may not have heard of. They include Leafcutter and Mason bees, Digger Bees and Carpenter Bees, Mining Bees and Stingless Bees (they bite instead!). Most of these are "Solitary bees". Unlike bumble and honeybees, they don't live together in a family group called a colony.

In this book, we are going to look mainly at honeybees. We'll find time to look at furry bumblebees too, like the one drinking nectar from the clover flower.

Honeybees are cold-blooded insects. They need the sun to warm them before they can fly and work.

They are clever creatures and live together in colonies; the colony's home is a hive. They are great organisers and have ways of talking to each other by smell and dance. You can learn about the waggle dance on page 18 and, on page 28, you will find a treasure hunting dance game.

Females run bee colonies.
It's a system known as a Matriarchal [from Latin Mater = Mother] society.

A bee's size depends on its type.

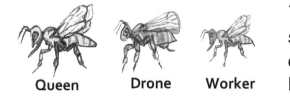

Queen   Drone   Worker

The biggest is the Queen,
second the Drone (a male)
and third the Worker who is female
but usually does not lay eggs.

They look the same, but there are important differences that allow them to do their individual jobs. Queen, drone and worker bee larvae have different diets.

LATIN

Apis mellifera Linnaeus
European honey bee

Apiarius   Beekeeper

Imker [German]

Biodlare [Swedish]

Colmenero [Spanish]

In 1735, Carl von Linné, a Swedish scientist, created a system for naming living things. It's called "Binomial nomenclature" and uses mostly Latin, but some Greek words too. The words describe the look or action of the part defined and we'll use them in this book. Using these words scientists can understand each other even if they speak different languages.

We can understand the importance of the system by looking at numbers. Everyone in the world uses the symbol 8 to represent EIGHT.

Here are some words that mean 8. Otte (Danish), Kahdeksan (Finnish) and Ocho (Spanish). If you are in a foreign country and want to buy candy bars, you can point at one and write 8. The shopkeeper will know what you want and how many. By using another number symbol he will write the price and you will understand that too.

On the blackboard are some Latin words. Apis means bee. Apis mellifera Linnaeus one of the World's most important honeybees originated in Europe. Using Latin and Greek like symbols for things in the natural world helps beekeepers in their work.

The Latin for Beekeeper is Apiarist. A German Imker, Swedish Biodlare and Colmenero from Spain (words for Beekeeper) understand Carl von Linné's system. They use it, like symbols, to name the parts of bees and their actions.

When there are new words I'll explain them and show their origin:
Latin (L) and Greek (G).

Wild bee scouts look for a new home for the colony. They explore trees, caves, roofs and cellars. When they find one they like, they tell the others by doing a dance. Then, worker bees make a hive (that's the name of the bees' house) out of wax. The queen moves into the new hive, and the colony follows.

Beekeepers know this and put a queen in the hive where they will keep a colony.

The hive is usually made from wood and has box sections that fit together. In each section there are 8 or more frames with a cell pattern. The bees use this pattern to create their honeycomb and it's the same pattern wild bees use. On a medium frame measuring 480 x

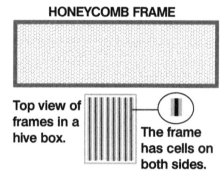

HONEYCOMB FRAME

Top view of frames in a hive box.

The frame has cells on both sides.

160 mm, worker bees build 2047 cells each side, that's 4094 on each frame. In one section, that can mean 32,752 cells!

There are two kinds of hexagonal cell. Honeycomb (average cell size 4.9 mm), for storing food, and broodcomb where the queen lays her eggs.

The broodcomb's cell types depend on the colonies needs for workers and drones. They

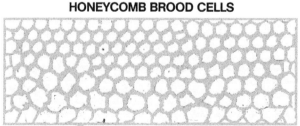

HONEYCOMB BROOD CELLS

The top small ones are for Workers.

The larger bottom ones are for Drones.

average 4.95 mm in size for workers and 6.18 mm for drones. The queen lays an egg according to the cell size. If a new queen is needed, workers make a special cell.

The queen will lay her eggs in any cell. To stop her, beekeepers make the entrance to upper sections of the hive so small that she can't enter. This keeps the upper section for honey.

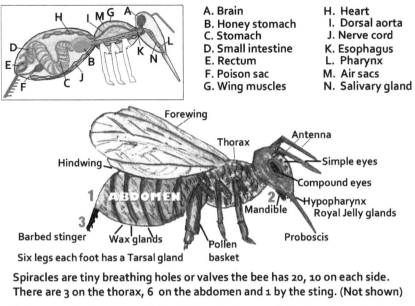

A. Brain
B. Honey stomach
C. Stomach
D. Small intestine
E. Rectum
F. Poison sac
G. Wing muscles
H. Heart
I. Dorsal aorta
J. Nerve cord
K. Esophagus
L. Pharynx
M. Air sacs
N. Salivary gland

Forewing
Thorax
Antenna
Hindwing
Simple eyes
Compound eyes
1 ABDOMEN
2
Hypopharynx
Mandible
Royal Jelly glands
3
Barbed stinger
Wax glands
Pollen basket
Proboscis
Six legs each foot has a Tarsal gland

Spiracles are tiny breathing holes or valves the bee has 20, 10 on each side. There are 3 on the thorax, 6 on the abdomen and 1 by the sting. (Not shown)

1. Nasanov gland   2. Mandibular gland   3. Koschevnikov gland

Glands produce pheromones, a chemical scent used to talk to other bees.

This is a worker bee's picture and description. They are the most important of the three.

Queens, workers and drones are distinct.

The queen can sting repeatedly with her straight stinger. She has a shorter proboscis and produces more pheromones.

Drones have a short proboscis, bigger eyes, and no stinger or honey stomach. They make the least pheromones of all three.

Bees are insects and do not have a skeleton. They have an exoskeleton, an outer one made from a material called chitin. It forms their wings too. Our nails and hair are made from a similar material called keratin.

I'll explain the new words on the next page.

When a worker bee drinks nectar, it goes down a tube that starts at the pharynx and mixes with saliva as it enters the esophagus. The worker eats some nectar, digesting it in the intestine and stores the waste in her rectum. The rectum is where poo collects until she poops.

Nectar, which the worker does not eat, is kept separately in its honey stomach. This nectar is used to make honey. Before adding it to the honeycomb, it adds an enzyme (that's a chemical), which helps to turn the nectar into honey.

Bee's blood is not like ours, but it does pump around the heart. The "Dorsal Aorta" is a pipe (known as an artery) that carries blood to the heart. They have a long nerve cord too. Bees do not have a nose or lungs, but breathe through Spiracles, which are holes in their sides.

NEW WORDS

Abdomen(L) = Belly

Antenna (L) = Sail Yard

Dorsal aorta (L) = Back /Pipe

Esophagus (G) = Gullet

Exoskeleton (G) = Outside skeleton

Hexagonal (G)= Six sided

Hypopharynx (G) = Under (the) throat.

Intestine (L) =Gut.

Mandible (L) = Jaw Chew

Ocelli (L) = Little eye

Ommatidia (G) = Eye

Pharynx (G) = Throat passage.

Proboscis (L) = Feeding tube.

Rectum (L) = End of large intestine.

Spiracles (L) = Breathing hole

Tarsal (L) = Foot, instep.

Thorax (L) = Breast Plate.

Learn how to say new words on page 24

Bees have five eyes! They have three simple eyes called ocelli, used for navigation. With them, they see Ultra Violet light (UV). Using UV they can see the sun through clouds.

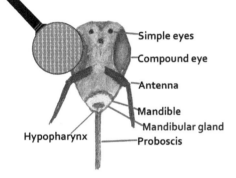

Simple eyes

Compound eye

Antenna

Mandible

Mandibular gland

Hypopharynx

Proboscis

Flowers use UV to guide the bee to nectar.

They have two compound eyes, which have between 5 and 10,000 ommatidia each. An ommatidium has 8 lenses. The bee uses these lenses, like a camera's pixels, to create a colour picture. Compound eyes have hairs growing on them, but as the bee gets older, the eye hair gets less.

Bees are good at seeing movement, so it's important to move slowly. When they're frightened, they sting.

The bee uses its jaws, instead of teeth to chew wood and shape wax. They can also clean other bees, bite pests (like mites) and, sometimes, other bees.

They drink water and nectar with the proboscis. They also use it to exchange food with other bees and for removing water from nectar.

Their antenna and feet are used to smell things. A bee's sense of smell is 100 times greater than ours. They also use their antenna to taste and feel.

Bees don't sleep, but do rest at night.

The Queen

The queen lays eggs of future queens in a specially made cell called a Queen cup. The cell is built over empty cells and, workers make it bigger as the larva grows. When the larva is ready to pupate, the workers seal the queen cup and it now looks like a peanut. In the bottom picture you can see the pupa.

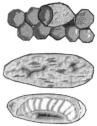

After a new queen cuts her way out of her cocoon, she cleans herself, drinks some honey and then makes a piping noise. This tells the hive she's arrived and that she'll fight other new queens. She will try to kill any she meets, and she looks for queen pupae and kills them too. Her sting is smooth and she can sting without hurting herself.

Between 6 and 10 days after coming out of her cocoon, she produces a scent called a pheromone. She uses this to attract a mate. She needs good weather for her mating flight, dry and warm so that she can meet lots of drones.

She stores the drone's sperm, using it all her life to fertilise her eggs. Three days after mating, she starts laying eggs. She lays about 1,600 a day, only stopping during cold months or when food is scarce. She lives for 3 to 4 years and may lay up to a million eggs in her lifetime.

The queen's job is to lay eggs and keep her colony together. After mating, she uses her pheromones to tell the workers what she needs. She tells them she's laying eggs, needs more food, more care or air-conditioning. All the time her scent is strong, the colony will protect and look after her.

The Drone

A hive has a few hundred drones, whose only job is to mate with the queen. They try hard to be handsome, so they will be chosen. Drones from many hives get together in special areas called "Drone congregation areas". There, they hang about, waiting for a queen. These areas are usually up to 1 km from their hive. Queens don't want to mate with drones from their own hive, and fly about 2 km, to meet ones from other hives.

Drone's eyes are twice the size of a worker, which help him to follow a queen as she flies. When a queen visits a drone congregation, she leads the drones 10 to 40 meters above the ground. There she mates with between 7 and 12 of them. She makes only one mating flight and stores the drone's sperm for use throughout her life. The drone's willy is called an "Endophallus" and, after he mates with a queen, it rips out of his abdomen and he dies. He may be handsome, but he's not as smart as the ladies!

Few drones mate and, when all the queens have mated, they have nothing to do. They don't harvest food, cannot clean and, because they don't have a stinger, are no good as soldiers. They can help with air-conditioning, but the workers do that anyway.

In a beehive, everyone has a job and those that don't have to leave. The worker bees put up with drones until they are sure the queen is fertile and healthy. Then they tell the drones to leave. The ones that don't take the hint, they pick up and throw out of the hive.

Drones have a short life, only about 4 months.

After the mating flight, the queen returns to her hive, and will rarely leave again. For the rest of her life, workers will keep her clean and feed her. Her only task is to lay eggs.

She lays an egg in each broodcomb cell and decides its sex, according to the cell's size. She uses stored sperm to fertilise the eggs that will become queens and workers. She does not fertilise drone eggs. Eggs measure about 1 mm and for 3 days the developing larva eats the yolk and loses weight. On day 3, it hatches. It looks like a tiny worm.

The larva eats, and eats and eats. Every 24 hours, it moults and sheds its old skin. It has to do this to make room because its skin does not stretch as it grows.

If you grew as much, you would be as tall as a Giraffe.

A moult is called an Instar, and after the 5th instar, the larva changes into a pupa. It does this by spinning a silk cocoon around itself. Then, workers seal the cocoon in its cell with wax.

The real magic, called metamorphosis (it means change), happens during its time in the cocoon. The pupa changes, growing legs, wings, eyes, mandibles and the other features that make it a bee.

The total time needed for the egg to develop into a bee is 16 days for the queen, 21 days for a worker and 24 for a drone. Of this time the cocoon stage lasts 8 days for a queen, 9 for a worker and 10 for a drone.

When metamorphosis is complete, the new bee cuts its way out of its cell, using its mandibles to bite through the wax seal.

MORE NEW WORDS

Instar (L) = Form or likeness Larva (L) = Ghost or mask
Metamorphosis (G) = Transform Pheromone (G) = To carry Pupa (L) = Doll

The Worker

98% of colonies are worker bees. They decide everything about life in the hive. From birth, they follow a program that will take them from cleaner to soldier and harvester.

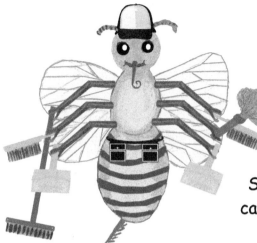

Worker bees have short lives, about six weeks, but those born in the autumn can live up to 5 months.

For the first two days of her life, the worker bee is a cleaner. Her first job is to clean herself. She is thorough, making sure that no bits of her larva case or beeswax are sticking to her.

Using her tongue and mandibles, she cleans and polishes used cells. Cells are re-used by the queen for laying eggs, and by older workers for food storage. She starts by cleaning her own cell and then moves to those nearby. The queen inspects each cell. If it's not clean enough, the worker bee has to clean it again, and again, and again, until the queen is happy.

Do you know

Removing dead larvae or bees is the last cleaning job. She pushes these to the entrance and older bees carry them away. This is an important job because it stops germs spreading that could make the colony sick.

During this time, she learns to cooperate with other bees working in teams to finish jobs.

Bees are fussy about hygiene and always poop outside the hive, so there are no toilets to clean. Bees need water and only pee tiny amounts, mixed with poop.

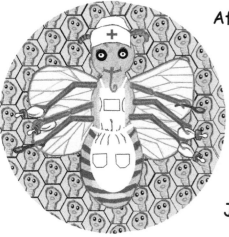

After 2 days, a worker bee starts to produce a food from glands in their hypopharynx. On day three she is promoted from cleaner to nurse. The nurse bee's first task is feeding older worker larvae with beebread. She makes it by mixing honey, pollen, water and her gland food. As a new worker bee, she eats this too.

After 5 or 6 days, her glands produce a special food, Royal Jelly. She is even busier now in charge of newborn larvae.

She organises their diet according to what they will grow into.

She knows what each egg will become from the size of the cell and from its smell. For the first two days, all larvae get royal jelly. Then it changes. From day 2 until they pupate, queen larvae are fed royal jelly. The diet of drone and worker larvae changes to beebread from day two.

Do you know

Nurse bee feeds the larvae up to 1,300 meals a day!

As she gets more experience, she will become a queen attendant. It's the worker attendant's job to feed and keep her clean whilst the queen concentrates on laying eggs.

She also feeds new drones. They are pretty useless, and take some time to figure out how to eat honey.

After about 10 days, the royal jelly gland stops working, and it's time for the worker to move to a new job.

11 days after coming out of their cocoons, worker bees start a whole new life. Excitedly, they make their first flight and learn how to find the way home by smell. But their life as a house bee is not yet over, there is more to do.

Workers make most beeswax when they are between 12 and 18 days old. It comes out of their wax glands as a liquid, but quickly hardens. The worker joins other workers, using wax to build brood and honey comb. Wax is also used to seal cells full of honey and to seal the cells of larvae when they pupate and spin cocoons.

The worker learns how to store the products older bees bring to the hive. These are nectar, water, pollen and propolis (also called bee glue). Propolis is used to make the hive waterproof and stop up holes.

They learn about air conditioning too. The best temperature for the hive is between 32 and 35 C. To achieve this, a team of workers use their body heat to warm the hive or they cool it by fanning with their wings.

Next, working in another team, they learn to make honey.

Forager bees mix nectar with an enzyme they make in their mouths, and then store it in their honey stomach. At the hive, they pass the treated nectar to a worker house bee. They take it into the hive where bees fan it with their wings. This process, called evaporation, reduces the water content.

Different types of nectar have varied sugar contents ranging from 4% to 65%. Honey has a sugar content of at least 80% and it can take a long time to evaporate the water. When it's thick enough, they add the nectar to a cell in the honeycomb. When it's full, the workers "Cap" the cell (seal it with wax) and the nectar ripens into honey.

Our worker's last job as a house bee is guard duty, as a soldier. All her other tasks have made her strong, and she joins soldier bees at the entrance to the hive. Here, she stands on four legs holding the front two up level with her mandibles. Now she is a bee on parade!

Her task is to inspect everyone who wants to enter the hive. She does this by checking their scent. You remember the tarsal gland? Every bee uses this gland to produce an oily footprint scent that tells the guards they belong to the colony.

That's why bees don't wipe their feet when they come home!

She will threaten any stranger, robber or wasp trying to get into the hive. First, she releases an alarm scent from her mandibular gland to scare them. If they don't leave, she will sting them. When she stings, she dies because the barbed sting stays in the invader and pulls out of her abdomen. Using her sting produces another alarm scent made by the Koschevnikov gland. This serious alarm signal alerts other soldiers. They continue the attack until the attackers die or run away.

Besides guarding the hive, she also flies patrols of the local area. The patrols try to stop threats before they happen.

Let's catch up on some new words we've just used.

Cocoon (L) = Shell
Enzyme (G) = leaven (Alter)
Koschevnikov gland = Makes alarm scent [discovered by scientist Grigorii Kozhevnikov]
Mandibular gland (L) = Gland in the jaw that produces alarm scent
Propolis (L) = Suburb. Word for resin called bee glue used to repair the hive.

Knowledge box

Before we follow the worker's life as a field bee, let's sum up and add some important points.

Worker bees are the real power and organisers of the colony's life in the hive. They are female but don't lay eggs. The queen makes a pheromone that stops them laying eggs and competing with her. It also makes them focus on their work.

 *Do you know* The workers may prevent a new queen fighting other queens. Indeed, they can keep her in prison by resealing a queen cup with wax. They do this to make sure their colony has a strong queen. One that can produce new queens, workers and drones. Not until a queen has had a successful mating flight will they accept her as the new boss. Even then they often protect the old queen until she dies a natural death.

After successfully mating, the queen determines the sex of the eggs she lays. Queens who do not mate successfully, lay eggs that all become drones. In this rare case, a worker bee will lay eggs that can become queens and workers. Then they kill the failed queen. That's a lot of murders isn't it? It sounds terrible to us, but we have to understand that in nature all that matters is survival. If only drones are born the colony will die out. The worker's task is to preserve her family and see it grow and she will do anything to stop it failing. Once they know the new queen is able to lay the eggs the colony needs, they will support and protect her.

During the winter honeybees cuddle around the queen to keep warm. In this tight bunch the workers are under the influence of her queen pheromone. In spring, the colony expands. Many new workers, unable to get close enough will not be under the queen's control. When this happens, the old queen will lead her followers in a swarm leaving the hive to a new queen. The swarm sends out scouts to find a new home and when they find one, they all move in. A typical hive has between 30 and 50,000 workers. Bees also swarm because of overcrowding.

Bees are not aggressive, but they can be nervous and will attack if they think they are under threat. Remember, give them space and move quietly.

Now lets follow our worker bee on her adventures outside the hive. As a field bee, she will have different responsibilities and new teams to work with. Her efforts will be vital in keeping the colony healthy and well fed.

She will get to fly long distances and explore new places.

Now, our worker bee is strong, well educated and ready for her next tasks. As a field bee, she needs new skills, including navigation (finding her way), scouting and harvesting. She will also learn how to tell other bees what she's found, and where it is.

Lets follow her as she goes on a typical foraging trip. She flies at about 25 km an hour beating her wings 200 times a second, that's 12,000 beats per minute! As she flies, her wing beats make the buzzing sound you hear. She will visit about 100 flowers each trip, and usually keeps within 2 km of the hive. Her main job is to collect nectar and pollen. If the hive needs them, she will also collect water and propolis. Propolis is a sticky substance from tree buds and sap that oozes from bark. Used for hive repairs, it's known as "Bee glue".

It takes 10,000 bees flying 85,000 km and visiting 2 million flowers to make 450 grams of honey. The taste and colour of honey depends on which variety of flowers bees harvest nectar from. Next time you are in a shop you can see this by looking at different jars. For example, jars with a label stating "Orange Blossom Honey" or "Lavender Honey". How many types can you list in your notebook? Worldwide, there are thousands of varieties. Individual countries will have from a dozen to a few hundred. A label that just states, "Honey" is a blend. Manufacturers make blends from many different honey types.

Do you know

Bees store nectar in their honey stomachs and pollen in their pollen baskets. In dry countries, they carry water to the hive too, sucking it into their proboscis. When our bee visits a flower it uses its ultraviolet sight.

We cannot see UV but bees can.

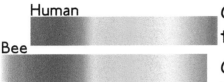

Human

Bee

On the left, are the colours we see, compared with those that a bee sees. They see more violet than us.

On the right, is a flower, to us it's yellow. For a bee it's violet, with lines guiding it to the pollen and nectar. Watch a bee land on flower. It goes straight to the middle - now you know why!

This is the inside of a flower. Wind pollinates about 10% of plants – grasses and wheat for example. A few plants and trees are either male or female like Holly trees (the ones with red berries are female). Others, like Squash, have separate male and female flowers growing on the same plant. But most plant's flowers are both male and female as in our picture. All these different types need insects like bees to fertilise them.

Look at the picture. You might think that this flower could just shake itself and the pollen would fall in the right place. That's not true. Also, it's healthier that a plant is pollinated by pollen from a different one. Self-fertilisation increases any defects and diseases the plant has.

Plants are clever. They know that the bee wants their sweet nectar, which, as you see, is at the base of the flower. To get it, the bee has to crawl past the anther, which is the male pollen producer. The pollen sticks to the bee and transfers to the stigma of the next flower it visits. It travels down the stigma and fertilises the seeds in the flower's ovule.

When the flower dies, the seeds dry out, get eaten by birds (and come out in their poo) or are blown by the wind. This way, they spread to fresh soil and become new plants.

Here are the new words we've learned about flowers.

Anther (L) = Medicine of flower (Pollen)
Filament (L) Thread (individual stalks)
Nectar (G) = Drink of the Gods
Nectaries (G) Where nectar is made
Ovary (L) = Egg or nut (*In plants, see page 24*)
Ovule (L) = Small egg (seeds)

Pistil (L) from pistillum = Pestle
Receptacle (L) = Storage space
Sepal (L) = Flower's leaf
Stamen (L) = Upright thread
Stigma (L) = Mark – Sticky top of Style
Style (G & L) Pillar = Stalk

Our worker's next job is scouting - for food, and sometimes, a new home. She searches for food by flying farther from the hive until she finds fresh flowers. It's rare, but bees are known to go as far as 8 km in search of food. Returning to the hive, she spreads the news by dancing. Austrian scientist Karl von Frisch discovered the dance and its meaning while studying honeybees.

The dance is called a waggle dance and she performs it on the honeycomb. Because bees can see UV light, she can use the sun's direction even on a cloudy day.

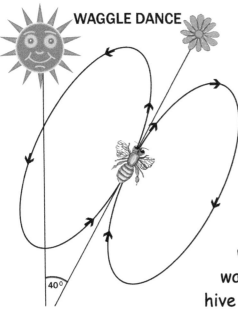

WAGGLE DANCE

Remember the honeycomb is vertical (upright). When she dances up it means toward the sun, dancing down means away from it. In our picture, she has found fresh flowers 40° to the right of the sun. She points along that line and starts her dance in a straight line. On the straight part, she waggles her bottom. Then she turns right making a circle, then straight again with a waggle before turning left. She repeats this pattern, waggle turn right and waggle turn left up to 100 times. Scientists think that the waggle time means distance, 1 second = 1 km. It's dark in the hive and the other bees have to touch her to feel her dance.

The sun moves across the sky, and the angle changes during the dance. Bees have an "Inner Clock" that lets them adjust the angle as they dance. Exactly how they do so is a mystery.

Our bee's last job is robbery! That sounds shocking, but in bee terms, it makes sense.

Experienced in every aspect of life and busy from the day she was born, she's smart enough to know how she can let others do the work before helping herself to their stores.

If there's a shortage of nectar, stealing by gangs of robber bees becomes a problem. They look for hives that are poorly guarded or have cracks where they can enter.

Hives with low populations are especially at risk because they have few soldiers. The guards and robbers may fight to the death. When they outnumber the guards, the robbers force their way past them or slip in unnoticed. Once inside, they help themselves to both honey and nectar. It is rare that they attack brood cells – all they want is food.

Our worker has had a busy career. She has had many different jobs and fitted them all into a short life. That's truly amazing!

Bees talk to each other in two ways. One way is dance and the other smell. We've already looked at some pheromones, but below and on page 20 is more detail about the main ones. Bees are complicated and produce many pheromones. There are books just about them if you want to study the subject.

Do you know

Larvae and pupae make a "brood recognition" scent that tells nurse if they will be workers or drones.

Drones make a scent to tell other males to meet them and hang around waiting for a queen. They also produce a footprint identifier with their tarsal gland.

Workers make scents that help them to do their jobs. As guards, they make two alarm pheromones. Like the others, they make an oily footprint recognition scent. As they grow older, they produce a forager pheromone that slows younger nurse bees' development. They do this so that the colony has the right number of cleaners, nurses, soldiers and foragers. They also make a scent called Nasonov pheromone used to guide bees back to the hive (or to the site of a new hive).

They distribute this scent by putting their bottoms in the air and fanning with their wings.

The queen makes the most and the strongest scents, she coats each egg with two of them as it's laid. The scent tells nurse that the queen laid the eggs. From her tarsal glands, she produces an oily scent that controls queen cell production. The queen mandibular pheromone (QMP) is one of the most important scents. It controls work in the hive and swarming. It also controls mating behaviour and stops worker bees laying eggs. The queen uses the "Queen Retinue Pheromone" to control the workers and make them care for and feed her.

Now, we are going to look at bumblebees. They are related to honeybees, but there are important differences. They are members of the family Bombus, but the English name is old. They are first mentioned in a book about fishing written in 1450 by a nun, Juliana Berners. She called them "Humblebees". This was not because they are shy or modest but because they make a "Humming" noise. By 1530, people decided the humm sounded more like bumble and called them "Bumblebees".

What do you think?

BUMBLEBEES

Pistils and stamens are set deep inside the flower of some plants, too deep for a honeybee to reach the nectar. Bumblebees are designed to deal with that. They have long tongues, in some species, almost as long as their bodies.

They hang upside down on the flower using their tongue to reach the nectar. Then, they vibrate their thorax, making the flower release its pollen. They pollinate some important plants. These are a few of the vegetables and fruit we enjoy thanks to bumblebees; aubergines, green peppers, tomatoes, blueberries and kiwis.

Bumblebees are just a bit longer than honeybees, but much heavier. They weigh up to 0.60 g compared to 0.10 for a honeybee; they are also furry and normally docile.

Bumblebee colonies are small, about 400 in general, but sometimes as few as 50. The queen lives for one year, the others live for just a few months and die in the late autumn.

A new queen survives by hibernating, usually in the earth. Before hibernating, she becomes extremely fat, gaining weight by eating lots of pollen and nectar. In the spring, she wakes up and searches for food. Once she has eaten, she finds a place to make a nest. This can be in a disused mouse burrow or under a shed – anywhere that seems dry and safe.

If you are lucky, you may see a queen in the early spring with her pollen baskets bulging. That means she's building a nest. Unlike *Do you* honeybees, our queen bumblebee has no help and has to forage *know* and create food stores alone. The queen's first job is to make a wax pot and fill it with nectar and pollen. Bumblebees don't make honey, but they do store nectar in cells.

After filling the pot, the bumblebee queen makes beebread, mixing pollen with nectar and saliva. She rolls this into a ball and covers it with wax. Onto this, she lays small batches of between 4 and 16 eggs. Then, like a bird, she sits on them to keep them warm.

By vibrating her thorax, she maintains a temperature of 30^0. That's why she needs her food pot because, until the eggs hatch, she can't leave them.

On average, the eggs hatch after 4 days. She makes individual cells for the larvae and feeds them pollen and some nectar. The time it takes to grow from egg to adult depends on the species and climate, and varies from 24 to 43 days. The larval stage lasts an average 11 days during which the larvae moult 4 to 5 times. Like honeybee larvae, they eat and eat, but do not poop storing it all inside them so they don't mess up the nest. After 11 days, the larva moults one last time, spins a silk cocoon, poops and becomes a pupa. The pupal stage, during which they change into a bee lasts about 12 days. Bumblebees don't make neat hexagonal honeycomb; in fact, their nests are a mess!

As soon as the first larvae have pupated, the queen will lay another batch of eggs.

The queen makes sure that all her children are workers to start with; she needs them to help in the nest. As the year develops, the colony grows. Towards autumn, the queen produces drones and queens.

The drones fly away to find new queens. The queens will find drones from other colonies with whom they mate late in the autumn. All the old bees, including the queen, die. The newly mated queens hibernate; ready to start again in the spring.

You may know that there is an exception to (almost) every rule. The bumblebee exception is the Buff-tailed bumblebee (Bombus terrestris). These bees sometimes stay awake all winter. They forage even when temperatures are low and there is snow on the ground.

Bumblebees don't swarm. If you see lots of them buzzing around, they are drones looking for a queen. Drones cannot sting, but queens and workers can. Unlike honeybees, they both have smooth stingers and can sting many times.

Bumblebees produce pheromones, but they do not dance. Their colonies are small, and they collect nectar and pollen near their nest. Unlike honeybees, there are no special house bees. They all work as house and field bees, collecting and storing nectar and pollen.

The cuckoo bee preys on bumblebees. As its name suggests it behaves like the cuckoo, laying its eggs on the brood ball. It may eat the real eggs or leave it to the larvae when they hatch. It looks like a bumblebee, has no pollen basket and is not as furry.

There are many creatures that prey on bees of all types. They range from mites (tiny insects) through to badgers and bears. Wasps and some types of spiders eat bees, as do birds. There is a bird called a 'Bee-eater' because it's so good at catching them. The biggest danger is from humans. We use pesticides, (chemicals to stop insects eating crops) but they kill bees too. Farmers are now trying to use other methods.

 *Do you know* To BEE safe with bees, there are a few simple rules. They are valuable little creatures and you must never hurt one. They will not hurt you unless they think you are threatening them. Move slowly as sudden movement is a danger signal. Do not poke a bee's nest or hive – if someone stuck a stick in your bedroom you'd probably bite them too!

Swarms are rare. If you see one, keep calm and warn those near by. Quietly, walk away and tell an adult.

More Latin!

Bombus (G & L) = Buzz   Hibernate (L) = Pass winter
Predator (L) = To rob   Terrestris (L) = Living on land

We've learned many new words and here is a guide to saying them.

Abdomen = Belly	Ab-doh-men	Ocelli = Little eye. (sg. Ocellus)	Oh-sel-eye
Antenna = Sail Yard (pl. antennae)	An-ten-nah	Ommatidia = Eye (sg. Ommatidium)	Om-uh-tid-ee-uh
Anther = Pollen	An-ther	Ovary = Egg. *	Oh-vuh-ree
Bombus = Buzz	Bomb-oos	Ovule = Small egg (seeds)	Oh-vyool
Cocoon = Shell	Ko-koon	Pharynx = Throat passage.	Far-inks
Dorsal aorta = Back - Pipe	Door-sul ey-awr-tuh	Pheromone = to carry.	Fer-uh-mohn
Enzyme = Alter	En-zahym	Pistil = Pestle (pl. Pistils)	Pisstel
Esophagus = Gullet	Ih-sof-uh-guhs	Predator = Robber	Pred-uh-tawr
Exoskeleton = Outside skeleton	Ek-soh-skel-i-tn	Probosci = Feeding tube.	Pro-boss-kiss
Filament = Thread	Fil-uh-muhnt	Propolis = Suburb.	Prop-uh-lis
Hexagonal = Six sided	Hek-sag-uh-nul	Pupa = Doll. (pl. Pupae)	Pew-puh
Hibernate = Pass winter	Hi-ber-neyt	Receptacle = Storage space.	Ri-sep-tuh-kuhl
Hypopharynx = Under (the) throat	Hiper-fa-rinks	Rectum = End of large intestine.	Rek-tum
Instar = Form or likeness	In-star	Sepal = Flower's leaf.	See-pull
Intestine = Gut.	In-tess-tin	Spiracles = Breathing holes.	Spy-ra-cull
Larva = Ghost or mask. (pl. Larvae)	Lahr-vuh	Stamen = Upright thread.	Stay-mun
Mandible = Jaw Chew	Man-de-bil	Stigma = Sticky top of Style.	Stig-muh
Mandibular = Gland	Man-deb-oolar	Style (G & L) = Stalk.	Sty-le
Matriarchal = Rule by women	May-tree-arkhel	Tarsal = Foot, instep.	Tar-sul
Metamorphosis = Transform	Met-uh-more-fuh-sis	Terrestris = Living on land.	Ter-res-tris
Nectar = Drink of the Gods	Nek-ter	Thorax = Breast Plate.	Thawr-aks
Nectaries = where nectar is made	Nek- ter-rees	pl. = Plural	sg. = Singular

Ovary is Latin and in Botany means Egg or Nut. It is the place that holds the ovule or seeds.
In humans and animals it refers to the place the eggs are made.

This guide is based on the way the words sound today. The modern way of saying them is different to the way we think the ancient Romans and Greeks said them. In Roman times, the latin R was a strong rolling RRRR sound and there were no letters J or W instead V sounded like W. U was OO and Th = T, which we still use in some names. Thames and Thomas for example. Latin is the basis of many modern languages and understanding it will help you in many ways.

HARVESTING HONEY.

Bees make 2 or 3 times more honey than they need and beekeepers are careful only to take the surplus. Each hive produces between 11 and 25 kg of honey, which is harvested in the autumn.

Harvesting is quite easy if you know what you are doing! The harvesters put on protective clothes, a veiled hat and gloves, making sure there's nowhere a bee can sting them. Next, they use a puffer to blow smoke into the top of the hive. This calms the bees so they don't produce alarm pheromones and make the whole hive crazy. The smoke does not hurt the bees.

The beekeeper inspects the honeycomb tray's cells, ensuring there are no larvae. They collect trays with at least 80% capped cells. (Workers cap cells with wax so that nectar ripens into honey). The beekeeper takes them to a special room. Here, the honeycomb is "Uncapped" by scraping a heated knife over the wax. The uncapped trays are put into a machine, called a centrifuge that looks like a drum. When full, the drum lid is closed and the inside spins around. The beekeeper turns a handle to work the small drum. Big machines have an electric motor. The spinning motion releases honey from the honeycomb and it drains off through a sieve into a bucket. Left behind is the honeycomb wax. Wax has many uses; furniture polish and candles are two examples.

The collected honey is now filled into jars and labelled – it's ready to eat!

All honey starts as "Runny Honey", over time it will set and can be unset by standing the jar in warm water. You can make creamed honey by churning 10% set honey with 90% liquid honey.

What's in Too Woo's bag?

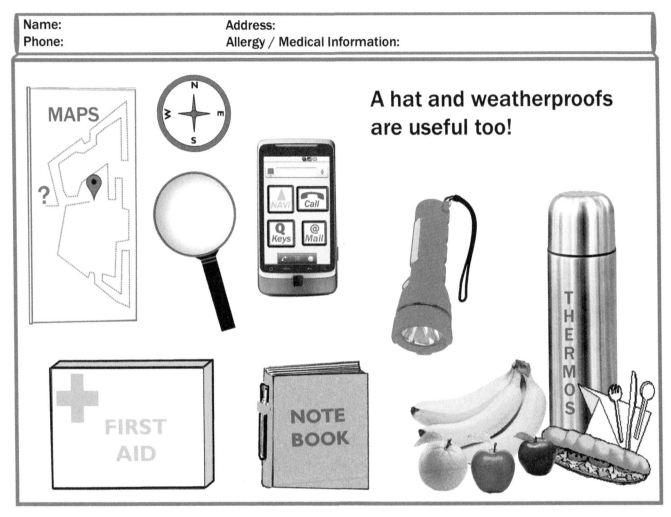

| Name: | Address: |
| Phone: | Allergy / Medical Information: |

MAPS

?

A hat and weatherproofs are useful too!

NAVi Call
Q Keys @ Mail

THERMOS

FIRST AID

NOTE BOOK

These items help you explore safely and avoid getting hungry or thirsty. You can add other things too.

Insect repellent, bite cream and antihistamine may be useful in your first aid kit. Ask an adult to pack your kit, make sure the contents are safe and that you know how to use them.

Oh yes, UV machines are used for lots of purposes (like killing germs). But they can be dangerous for humans. They are not toys.

QUIZ

01. What does the bee carry from flower to flower?
02. What was the Roman goddess of honey's name?
03. How many types of plant do bees pollinate?
04. What do you wear thanks to bees?
05. How many species of bees are there in the world?
06. Can you name 4 of them?
07. What is a bee family called?
08. What is the bees home called?
09. Which bee is the biggest?
10. What did Carl von Linné invent?
11. What is the Spanish for eight?
12. How do you write 8 in Spanish?
13. What are the two types of honeycomb?
14. What is broodcomb used for?
15. Can all bees sting?
16. How many eyes do bees have?
17. What can bees see that we can't?
18. How many eggs might a queen lay in her life?
19. What is a drone's job?
20. What are the two phases of a worker bee's life?
21. Can you name three of the house bee's jobs?
22. How fast can bees fly?
23. What do worker bees harvest?
24. How many bees are needed to make 450 gm of honey?
25. What do scout bees do?
26. How do bees talk to each other?
27. What is bee scent called?
28. What special features do bumblebees have?
29. What do bumblebees share with birds?
30. What is the machine called that takes honey out of the tray?
31. How is creamed honey made?

There are lots of questions and you can try answering a few at a time.
It's not a competition, but a way to help you learn.

Answers are on page 31

WAGGLE DANCE

Tell a group of friends where you have hidden flowers or treats (the treasure) by doing the waggle dance. The dance rules are on page 18.

When you've hidden the treasure, measure how far away it is from your starting point. You can decide what each complete waggle movement equals, for example 2 meters.

2   1

Explain the rules. Say what distance a waggle equals. They have to watch where you point before you start your dance. They must count the number of waggles. When you stop, they can find the treasure.

Do the bottom waggle. From straight go left, then through straight, go right, then back to straight for one complete waggle.

Copy the waggle girl's movement.

Remember, each waggle of your bottom from left to right equals the measure of length you've decided.

For example: 5 waggles x 2 meters = 10 meters.

Don't forget, only waggle on the straight.

28

Please help! This is her first day as a field bee and she can't see anything, there is no colour. Please paint the picture.
There's a butterfly who's lost too.

29

Here are flowers for you to colour.

Can you paint the top two the way you see a flower and bottom ones the way the bee does?
You can look at page 17 before you start.

QUIZ ANSWERS

01. Pollen
02. Mellona
03. 250,000
04. Jeans
05. 25,000
06. Honeybee, bumblebee, Masonbee, Diggerbee
07. A Colony
08. A hive
09. The Queen
10. A naming system for living things
11. Ocho
12. 8
13. Super and broodcomb
14. The queen lays eggs and the larvae and pupae develop in it.
15. No. Drones cannot sting.
16. Five.
17. Ultraviolet (UV) light.
18. Up to a million.
19. To mate with the queen
20. House bee and field bee.
21. Cleaner, nurse, builder, honey maker and soldier.
22. 25 km per hour.
23. Nectar, pollen, propolis and water.
24. 10,000.
25. Look for flowers or a new home.
26. With scent and dance
27. Pheromone.
28. A very long tongue and they can vibrate their thorax.
29. They sit on their eggs.
30. A centrifuge.
31. By mixing 10 % set honey with runny honey and churning it.

ABOUT THE AUTHOR

In writing the Too Woo series I set out to try and right a wrong that irritated me as a child. Adults often treated my questions as a nuisance. Answering, "That's why" or "You are too young to understand." Of course, I was a child, but thought that my questions deserved an answer. Towards the end of my school career, I realized that I was asking questions for which adults had no answer. It was not until I started work that I met someone who said, "I don't know, but let's find out". Joy!

In the "The magical world of butterflies", I tried to ask and answer the questions that would have interested me as a child. This book continues that theme. Reviewers of the first book have been most kind with their comments. I hope they find this a worthy successor.

I'm busy cooking, writing and painting. But I'm more than ever convinced that childish curiosity is essential for a happy life and refuse to grow up. I am still as curious as when I was young. I live my life believing that going to bed without having learned one new skill or fact, during that day is a day wasted.

WEB SITES

The British Beekeepers Association, founded in 1874, is one of the oldest bee societies in the world. They have information for children also about bee friendly gardens. http://www.bbka.org.uk/

The Bumblebee Conservation trust is a great resource about bumblebees. http://bumblebeeconservation.org/

Bee-equipment Ltd is a UK based company specialising in beekeeping and honey production. Lots of information on their website. http://www.bee-equipment.co.uk/

In the US, West Plains Beekeepers Association (Washington state) is an organisation that teaches and trains beekeepers. It has a very good "Resources" section http://www.wpbeekeepers.org/

BOOKS

The Bee-Kind Garden: Apian Wisdom for Your Garden by David Squire, published by Green Books, ISBN-13 9780857840240. Information about bees and gardens.

Guide to Bees and Honey by Ted Hooper, published by Northern Bee Books, ISBN: 9781904846512. Written in 1976, it is still considered the most comprehensive book on the subject, and is a best seller.

Beeswax Alchemy: by Petra Ahnert, published by Rockport Publishers Inc, ISBN-13 9781592539796. A great book about beeswax and the things you can make with it.

My Notes

You can use the notebook for different things. Where you saw the first honeybee or bumblebee of spring. The flower (s) they visit and how often. Don't forget the different types of honey too.

DATE	WHERE	WHAT

Lightning Source UK Ltd.
Milton Keynes UK
UKOW07f0756300417

300182UK00008B/37/P